The Minimalist And Decluttering Lifestyle

Use Minimalism to Declutter Your Home, Mindset, Digital Presence, And Families Life Today For Living a More Fulfilling Minimalistic Lifestyle With Less Worry!

By Samuel Newell

Table of Contents

Introduction

Congratulations on acquiring *The Minimalist And Decluttering Lifestyle* and thank you for doing so.

The following chapters will discuss many areas of this topic, starting with the definition. We will dive into a brief history of this movement and its core concepts. This book will also show you why decluttering is so beneficial to emotional and mental well-being and why you should adopt it into your own life.

After reading this book, you will also begin to understand the larger culture of consumerism in which we live and why it has left so many of us unhappy. You will learn how minimalism can be an antidote to this shallow, hyper-consumeristic society. Once we've dived into the philosophy underlying this idea, we will begin to introduce practical guidance on how you can declutter your home room by room.

Not only will you learn to declutter your physical spaces, but you will learn to declutter your mental spaces as well. As a society, we fill our minds with ceaseless chatter that take up valuable real estate in our brains and prevent us from being fully present in each moment. Once you've learned to declutter your mind, this work will show you how to go one step farther and declutter your life. Decluttering your life allows you to make space for those things that truly matter.

The final part of this book will walk you through how not to fall off the wagon and ensure that you can translate this philosophy into a sustainable, long-term lifestyle.

There are plenty of books on this subject on the market. Thanks again for choosing this one! Every effort was made to ensure it is full of as much useful information as possible. Please enjoy!

Chapter 1: What is Minimalism?

The best place to start is at the beginning. This chapter is going to provide you with a basic outline of what minimalism is all about. First, we're going to spend some time defining the term and also going into a brief history of the word as it has been used across music, lifestyle, and art. We will trace the origins of this method through ancient Greek philosophers and millennia-old spiritual traditions. We will learn about how minimalism is used today and why people are turning to the movement.

The minimalist lifestyle is defined as living with fewer possessions. However, contrary to popular misconceptions, it's not about living in an empty apartment with one chair and a single coffee mug. Quite to the contrary: it's about eliminating things from your life that you don't actually need, which gives you the ability to base your life around experiences rather than possessions.

The word minimalism comes with a lot of baggage. People hear it and immediately think that you can't own a car or house, must travel the world and live out of a backpack and that you must deprive yourself of things that you love. Minimalism isn't about getting rid of things that you love. It's about getting rid of extraneous "stuff" that just clutters up our lives. In the space you then create, you are more fully able to appreciate the belongings that genuinely ignite joy in you. This philosophy, at its core, is about value—keeping the things we truly value and getting rid of the things we don't.

The term "minimalism" was indirectly coined by Robert Wollheim, an art critic who was attempting to come up with a way to describe a new aesthetic that was sweeping through the art world at the time. The actual word he used was "minimal art-content," though, eventually, this clunky phrase was streamlined into the "-ism" we know and use today.

The movement has some of its most ancient roots in the writings of the ancient Greek philosopher Epicurus, who wrote that a happy life was an untroubled life and that an untroubled life was obtained through careful consideration regarding where one spent one's time and energy. Epicurus's main thesis on this point stated that the challenges of maintaining a lifestyle of extravagance largely outweighed the joy one receives from that lifestyle in the first place. Henry David Thoreau was another famous minimalist who wrote about his experiences with simple and sustainable living in his book *Walden.* Thoreau's time on the shores of Walden Pond permeates the American literary consciousness when scholars ponder the ideas of simplicity and mindful living.

Minimalism is also the name of an artistic movement that swept through the scene of the 1950s and 1960s. This movement was characterized by its streamlined, usually massive, and extremely simplistic forms. The goal of the art medium was to allow the mind to find purchase on the essential nature of the piece by removing all frills, bells, and whistles.

Famous minimalist artists included Donald Judd, Frank Stella, Sol Lewitt, Carl Andre, and Eva Hesse. One well-known modern minimalist is Yayoi Kusama, a Japanese artist who was renowned for her unique polka-dot painting style. All of these artists used the pared-down viewpoint of this philosophy to create unique, stunning works of art.

While the art form may seem unrelated to the lifestyle, in essence, they both capture the same spirit: allowing the human mind to peer deeply into the nature of something (be it a piece of art or one's own life) to find its true value and meaning.

Perhaps, the most ancient roots of minimalism, though, go back to the world's religious traditions. It was a tenant of some of the earliest documented religious traditions such as the Sramana sect of India's Iron Age as early as 1200 BCE. Ancient figures such as the Buddha and the Nazarites of the Bible also espoused a belief that fewer belongings, and therefore, fewer attachments to the material world allowed space in one's mind for spiritual contemplation. For these spiritual leaders and founders, making physical space in their lives made metaphorical space for spiritual connection.

One of the most profound influences on the modern Minimalist movement has been the teachings of the Zen Buddhist tradition. The very foundations of the Zen Buddhist tradition and Buddhism in general, lead minimalism to be a natural outgrowing of their spiritual philosophy. At its core, this set of spiritual traditions demands that adherents let go of attachments and increase the mindfulness in their everyday lives.

From the ancient past to today, this philosophy is alive and well. There are many people who have become famous by documenting their minimalist lifestyle online, such as Leo Babauta. People are becoming increasingly more restless nowadays to find some kind of true meaning in their lives and getting increasingly stressed out by the burden of stuff.

Some people are abandoning the traditional trappings of success altogether and are moving into vans and traveling the country. Others are reducing the size of the space in which they live to save both money and mental energy, which is one of the reasons behind the tiny house craze that has popped up in recent years. However, many other people are living in perfectly normal-sized apartments and houses, but are still paring down the number of possessions they own.

Minimalism and decluttering are having a moment in the sun due to the booming popularity of a certain Netflix special about tidying up your home. Despite the philosophy's current fad status, there is a real opportunity for growth and increased happiness found in this lifestyle.

There are many reasons that people become minimalists. Not everyone has the desire to become a

Buddhist monk and to abandon all of their attachments to material belongings. You may want to live in a tiny home and figure out how to reduce your amount of possessions to fit in that space. Or you may have a normal-sized home and simply find yourself stressed and unhappy. Either way, decluttering can help you find fulfillment and get in touch with what you truly value in life.

Chapter 2: Why Declutter?

Now that we have established a definition, briefly explored the term's context in art and culture, and outlined its secular and spiritual origins, we can attend to the pressing question: why declutter at all?

This chapter will spend time outlining the reasons that we accumulate "stuff" in the first place and the psychology of extraneous belongings. Among these reasons are the need to appear successful to people, the feeling of security that owning things can bring, and the fear of scarcity that causes us to hang onto things that we just don't need.

This chapter will then go onto exploring the negative effects on mental health that clutter brings to our lives, and then we'll provide information regarding the mental health benefits that a clutter-free space can bring.

Why we accumulate "stuff"

In American society and Western society at large, we have certain lessons drilled into us from the time we're young. In order to be considered successful in the eyes of our peers and in the eyes of our culture, we need to own certain things. The clearest rendition of this dream is a large suburban house with a white picket fence, a purebred golden retriever in the yard, and one (preferably two) shiny new cars parked in the driveway.

When people don't know what they truly value or want in life, they default into living their lives for other people, not for themselves. If they don't know what they want, then they seek to acquire what everyone else says they should want. The problem with this is they end up with a life full of very expensive things, a large amount of debt, and very little happiness.

Aside from mindlessly acquiring things to meet arbitrary societal standards of success, we also acquire things due to the feeling of security that having many physical belongings can bring us. Being surrounded by stuff, especially expensive and trendy stuff can make us feel good about ourselves and our lives. Just as animals build nests to sleep in, humans also build spaces to rest and fill it with things to make themselves comfortable. There is a fine line, though, between a comfortable couch on which to rest and thirty different throw pillows to go on that couch.

The final reason that we accumulate belongings is because of a culturally-programmed fear of scarcity. We are not only trained to believe that in order to be happy we must accumulate many belongings, but are also trained to believe that the opposite is true: that poverty is humiliation because the poor are not able to purchase indiscriminately as part of the endless cycle of consumption.

As members of a culture, we are trained to believe that being poor is one of the worst things that we can be. And being poor is associated with a lack of belongings. Therefore, in order to avoid looking and feeling poor, we accumulate many different kinds of belongings—many of which we do not actually need. Obviously, there are many levels of incorrect reasoning, but the ultimate effect is the same. People end up with a home full of stuff they don't actually need due to a deeply ingrained cultural fear of what would happen if they gave up all their stuff.

Clutter and mental health

To put things simply, the clutter in your outer space is a direct reflection of the clutter in your inner space. People who have a lot of superfluous items taking up space in their house tend to have more chaotic minds and feel less in control of their lives. Have you ever walked into someone else's space and felt immediately stressed out by all of the belongings piled up everywhere? Now, imagine living in that constant state of stress. Even if the number of belongings we've accumulated aren't on the level of a hoarding situation, the increased amount of items taking up space in your visual field increases stress levels.

Several scientific studies have been done on this topic and have introduced a term that helps to talk about this topic: "mental hygiene." This is a more technical and official way of talking about mental clutter. People who have a large number of belongings in small spaces have been shown to have higher stress responses in general and to feel less rested in their home spaces.

The number of items in a home takes up space in the visual field. When there are a large number of items in the visual field, the mind is far less efficient at visual processing. This, in turn, means that your brain has to work twice as hard just to understand what it is looking at.

Not only does it lead to less efficient visual processing, but clutter also leads to less efficient thinking in general. Due to the elevated stress levels that people living with cluttered homes feel, their brains have to work far harder just to perform basic tasks when compared to normal people. This stress can lead to exhaustion, fatigue, and unhappiness. Living in clutter was also shown in a scientific study to cause people to make worse dietary choices. When people feel overwhelmed, they are more likely to eat food that is convenient and comforting, which has further negative effects on their health.

In short, there are many reasons that clutter is bad for you. From a purely practical standpoint, clutter makes it harder to move around your home and to find what you're looking for. A deeper and more concerning problem, though, is the way that clutter makes us less mentally and physically healthy. Getting rid of excess stuff can not only help you gain peace of mind but may also add years back onto your life.

Benefits of Decluttering

We've spent a lot of time in this chapter describing why clutter is bad for you. But the act of decluttering doesn't need to be approached from a place of fear and the desire to avoid negative consequences to physical and mental health. Though of course, these are helpful motivators. There are many positive benefits that the principle of minimalism can bring to your life. So then, let's answer the question: why declutter?

The simplest answer is that it will improve your life. There are many people and regimens out there that promise a "magic pill" or "magic bullet" that will solve your problems and fix your life. These regimens make outlandish promises and almost always fall short, but they are attractive because they make the promise that you won't have to do any work to improve things.

One of the biggest benefits that people report feeling after decluttering is a new sense of freedom. When people release their attachment to so many unnecessary belongings, they finally feel unshackled. They realize that they didn't own their belongings; their belongings owned them. Uncoupling themselves from items that didn't bring true value into their lives allowed them to gain an immediate and profound sense of relief.

After decluttering, people also reported profoundly increased metrics of happiness and satisfaction with their lives. When they removed the stressors of excess belongings, their homes stopped feeling like an enemy and became the restful refuge they were supposed to be in the first place.

The physical act of decluttering also helps you to identify which items truly bring you joy. By getting rid of everything that does not bring true value into your life, you are only left with those things that improve the quality of your life. By getting rid of these excess items, you are also able to answer the big questions: what do you truly value in your life? And then you can put your focus into those areas. This is a great way to rediscover and refine your passions.

Someone may have a home full of novelties and collectibles of trains. They may have railroad signs, model trains, pictures, posters, and other flotsam. They may also have a camera. Through the act of decluttering, they may discover that the thing that really brings them joy is the act and hobby of capturing different kinds of trains on films. They can remove all of the extraneous flotsam, but keep the camera. In this case, they have discovered the heart of minimalism: finding the heart of the thing that brings you happiness, keeping those items, and getting rid of the rest.

Not to mention that this philosophy is also great for your wallet. When you realize what you truly value, you avoid purchasing items you don't actually need or want. When you avoid purchasing excess items, that money stays in your wallet, giving you greater financial stability. Finally, it's also great for the environment. If you're purchasing fewer items, your carbon footprint is immensely smaller.

Clutter is just plain bad for you. You trip over it in your home and it makes what should be a place of refuge a place of stress, and it becomes more of a pain to clean. Aside from the purely logistical issues, clutter also makes you less mentally healthy. It raises the level of stress hormone in your system and decreases the processing efficiency of both your eyes and your brain. By abandoning clutter and taking up the philosophy of minimalism, though, your mental hygiene is drastically improved. People who embrace minimalism find not only cleaner homes, but also greater satisfaction with their lives, and a better ability to understand who they are and what they value in life.

Chapter 3: Minimalism in the World of Stuff

Thus far, we've outlined the definition and history of minimalism, as well as why people should take up this philosophy. This chapter will take you on tour through the American cultural underbelly that so many of us have neglected to examine. It will lay bare several cultural assumptions that cause us to accumulate so many things that we just don't need. Once we've revealed the details of this cultural programming, this chapter will define how the minimalist philosophy directly counteracts that programming. We will also explore how that cultural programming plays out on the level of the individual and the harmful beliefs it has ingrained into us, as well as how we can use minimalism to begin to heal from those harmful societal beliefs.

Western Society, Capitalism, and Consumerism

The basis of our society is capitalism, and its natural outgrowth, consumerism. First, let's go over a few definitions. Capitalism is defined as an economic system that is controlled by private owners for profit. In capitalism, profit is the king. The goal, then, is to generate as much profit as possible. In order to do this, private companies have ceaselessly advertised and tricked people into purchasing more and more items. This is consumerism.

When the economy is based on capitalism, the goal is to generate ever-increasing amounts of money. In order to generate ever-increasing amounts of money, companies need to sell ever-increasing amounts of goods and services. And consumers must constantly buy these new goods and services. This economic system is flawed for two reasons. First, it assumes an infinite amount of resources from the Earth from which to create new goods and services; of course, we know the Earth's resources are finite. Secondly, it assumes that consumers have an infinite amount of space in their homes and lives to fill with stuff.

This second flaw in the design of our economic system has led us to fill our homes with ever-increasing amounts of stuff, while the amount of room we have has stayed the same. Or worse, we are tricked into buying or renting larger homes so that we can fit all of the stuff we've accumulated. Perhaps most devastating of all, we, as a society, have been lured onto a treadmill of endless, mindless consumption. The term "retail therapy" has emerged to describe how people attempt to find stress relief from the purchasing of items; ironically, those same items cause yet more stress as they pile up in people's homes.

Without consumers constantly purchasing new goods and services, the system falls apart. So, in the name of self-preservation, the system has to work very hard to continue convincing us to continue to purchase new items. The economy would go into freefall tomorrow if everyone were to suddenly decide that they didn't need a new car or a new television, or that they could simply repair something that was broken, rather than purchasing a shiny new gadget.

There is a finite number of things that humans need to have all of their basic needs met. On a purely functional level, once we've acquired the basics that we need for survival and some degree of comfort and self-realization, we really don't need any more items. The job of these companies, then, is to convince us otherwise. They do this by hijacking our sense of well-being and safety, causing us to believe that if we do not possess these items, then our life will not be as safe, happy, or fulfilled.

The damages of this hijacking are threefold. Firstly, there is the excessive stuff that crams our home and causes us stress. Secondly, there is the damage to our mental health and sense of self-esteem from being constantly assailed by advertising and media. Thirdly, there is the effect of resource depletion on the Earth that our endless consumption drives. In the last hundred years, humans have killed off sixty percent of the animal wildlife, cut down more than half the Earth's trees, and done extensive damage and pollution to the world's oceans, rivers, and landscapes—all in the name of profit, to feed the cycle of consumerism.

We live in a society that believes, by and large, that getting rich and having many possessions will automatically make someone happy. Don't get me wrong, having enough money to pay for food, shelter, healthcare, and other basic necessities greatly reduce the stress of living. But the consumer mindset is a different animal entirely. Despite the common cultural maxim that "money can't buy you happiness," no one really seems to believe it.

Because we have learned to equate belongings with happiness, we don't know how to be happy without belongings. Many people can't even imagine how they could be happy without all their stuff. This has led us down a rabbit hole of forgetting how to be happy, and where the true source of happiness lies.

This is where the idea of minimalism turns the corner from simply a method of getting rid of stuff to a full-on philosophy that you can use to live your life. Our society has been so successful in convincing us that we need to purchase things to be happy, that we have forgotten how to make themselves happy without purchasing things.

So what is the true source of happiness?

The true sources of happiness are things that seem so glaringly obvious that, to most people, they seem banal. When people are on their deathbeds, their regrets don't center on wishing they had purchased more material belongings. The five most common deathbed regrets are striking in their simplicity. Dying people wish they hadn't worked so hard and spent more time with the people they care about. They wish that they had the courage to express their feelings. They wish that they had made time for the people who were important to them. Most crucially to our point here, they wish that they had had the courage to live their lives the way they truly wanted, rather than living to uphold other people's expectations or follow the script our society has laid out for us.

Minimalism is a way to prevent yourself from ending up with these regrets because it is how to depart from the societal script and rediscover the things that truly matter.

How cultural programming affects you (900)

By virtue of growing up in a society, we are programmed by the expectations of that society. Many people never realize it. It is similar to how a fish may never realize that it is swimming in water. When you are immersed in something, it can be difficult to perceive it. This unseen force causes us to feel insecure, constantly needing to prove ourselves, and measuring our worth by other people's standards of success.

Insecurity

In order to keep us purchasing items that we don't need, the media machine has worked tirelessly to convince us that we need their products. How, though, do you convince someone that they need your product? Well, there are a few ways to do this. There is the element of "FOMO," or "fear of missing out" that brands seek to create in their advertising. This makes people believe that they are missing out on crucial life experiences or that their lives are not as vibrant or fulfilled if they do not have the products being displayed on the screen.

A car company may show some sleek, fit young people driving down a highway in a convertible and pulling up to a party. The subliminal message being that your life is boring and uneventful and that if you want the kind of happiness being displayed on the screen, then you need to purchase the car. Of course, the car won't bring you the experience, but we are tricked into spending tens of thousands of dollars on the mistaken belief that it will.

Another way that companies prey on our insecurities is by making us think that we are not good enough unless we have their products. This is especially true in African American communities, where fairer skin is equated with beauty; this has led to a boom in the sale of skin-bleaching kits. These products are painful and dangerous, but advertising and cultural forces tell women that unless their skin is lighter, that they are ugly.

Cosmetic products—and any product marketed at women, really—are perhaps the biggest perpetrators of this negative trend. The entire industry makes bank by convincing women that they are not thin enough, that they are not pretty enough, and that they are not good enough. But with the purchase of this miracle product, they can be! And once they have the product, they will be beautiful, and once they are beautiful, they will be happy.

Except, we all know that this isn't how it really works.

Proving Ourselves

The companies that rule the media landscape in which we live, drill insecurity into us from a young age. Because people feel insecure, they are left with the constant urge to prove themselves. This is especially true among the men of Western culture. They need to prove their power, strength, social status, and ability to attract a mate, lest they are made objects of ridicule.

The metrics of success that our society provides us with are a double-edged sword. Firstly, people internalize the belief that they need to own certain things in order to be happy. Secondly, they harshly judge other people who don't own those things. In the end, it's not just the companies convincing us to buy things; social pressure and fear of judgment for not owning a certain item also contribute to people's purchasing habits.

Imagine a hypothetical man working at an office. Everyone around him has a high-end car, and his used, dented vehicle sticks out like a sore thumb in the parking lot. He hasn't purchased a new car because he has a significant amount of student loan debt and finances are tight. However, he begins to feel the pressure as his coworkers joke about his car. Even though he isn't quite able to afford it, he gives in and takes on a significant amount of new debt so that he doesn't feel insecure anymore.

When we are pushed around by the peer pressure and social judgment of the people around us, we end up making decisions based on other people's ideas of how we should be living, rather than how we truly want to live. This is also a way of life that is rooted in avoiding pain, judgment, and alienation. It is a way of life rooted in avoiding what is negative, rather than a way of life rooted in seeking out what is positive.

There are many traditional markers of success that society tells us we need to have in order to be considered stable and successful. Homeownership and (new) car ownership are two of the big ones. But there are other smaller markers as well. These include the latest fashions; purebred, designer pets; a television of a certain size; and many other kinds of upscale items.

If we don't have these things, then society tells us that we've failed. What's worse is that we've become so conditioned into believing that we need these things for success that we also begin to believe that we've failed. In truth, we've merely been operating by someone else's standards of success.

The beauty of minimalism is that it allows you to finally take back control of your own life. You are able to stop defining your life by other people's standards of success and begin to discover what success means to you. Everyone has a different definition because everyone's life and happiness are rooted in different things.

One of the most valuable things minimalism can teach you is how to begin to live your life for yourself rather than for other people. Those regrets that people have on their deathbed almost always stem from merely following the external forces of one's life, rather than consciously deciding to move through the current. It is difficult to decide to change one's relationship to material possessions, especially when we live in a society that has taught us to judge and be judged by others when they don't own certain things. Cultivating a minimalist lifestyle is ultimately also an act of compassion—not only for other people as you stop judging them but also towards yourself, as you free yourself from a life that was never truly yours, to begin with.

Chapter 4: How to Declutter Your Space

Decluttering can seem like a lot of work, and it can be—but it doesn't have to all be done at once. And in the process of decluttering, you'll begin to discover more than just more floor space. You'll begin to find a deeper appreciation for your belongings and a greater appreciation for your life at large. Now that we've discussed the philosophical underpinnings of the idea of minimalism, it's time to move on to some practical steps to help you declutter your home. This chapter will provide guidance on how to declutter six different areas of the home, including living rooms, kitchens, bedrooms, closets and clothing, and storage areas.

A note on being overwhelmed

When you're staring down the barrel of the decluttering gun, it can seem extremely intimidating. Looking around your home, you may not know where to start. As with any major journey, such as deciding to get in shape, to change career, or start a new business, the sheer size of the task ahead may make people freeze up—it may cause so much anxiety that they never get past the starting line.

There are a few tips to help you take the first step on your journey. First things first, breathe! Don't psyche yourself up before you try to start decluttering. Try to pick a day when you are in a relaxed state of mind to start decluttering and living the minimalist lifestyle.

Secondly, take things one thing at a time. You don't need to get everything done at once. You don't have to tackle your entire house in one day. Just pick one room. And then in that room, pick one space, like a bookshelf or a coffee table. When you're just beginning, even a little progress is a lot of progress.

Thirdly, remember that the attitude you're cultivating along the way is just as important as the physical act of cleaning. Even if it seems like the piles of stuff will never get sorted out, just take a moment and realize that you're doing major work not only in your environment but also in your own mind. So, really, you're doing double the amount of work, except that half of it is going on in your head.

Fourthly, take breaks. You don't have to have one marathon session where you get everything done in a blazing streak of productivity. Break it up into smaller chunks. Productivity science shows us that our attention span is able to focus on one task for forty minutes to an hour at most. After that hour, take a brief break. That break will help to downplay the stress and keep you refreshed enough to keep going.

Finally, make it fun! If you're looking at this task like a high schooler looking at their geometry homework, it's going to be so much harder to get it done. Maybe you could invite a friend over, and you could reminisce over the items you're sorting. You can tell funny stories as you declutter. And, of course, no one ever said that you had to do your decluttering when you were one hundred percent sober. That said, don't get too crazy. You still want to have the presence of mind to make some hard decisions.

With all that said, let's dive in!

Living room

The living room is where we spend most of our downtime. Thus, it's natural that it would accumulate a diverse array of flotsam from almost every domain of our lives. Whether we're sitting on the couch watching a movie, on the floor playing with our children, or gathered around the table engrossed in a board game, or just snuggled up and enjoying a good book, many different activities happen in this room. However, that also makes it a prime location to dump hockey skates when you're in a rush, throw down your umbrella, or leave that half-done craft project. So, how do you handle this room?

Start with one drawer

This bit of advice harkens back to the fact that it's extremely easy to feel overwhelmed by this process. Thus, it makes sense to start with an objective that is small, contained, and easy to finish. Once you finish, you'll have a solid sense of accomplishment that you will be able to use to keep the momentum going.

Depending on the contents of the drawer, your organizational system will vary from drawer to drawer. However, a general note is that you should be able to easily find what you're looking for with a glance when you open it. Put anything you don't use into a pile and organize the rest. You may want to consider obtaining rubber bands to secure loose cords, which can easily get tangled when shoved inside of a drawer. You may also want to consider obtaining small baskets or dividers to help you organize the contents of your drawers.

Flat surfaces

Clear off any and all flat surfaces. This includes the couch, the coffee table, the top of the bookshelf—everything. Flat surfaces are like magnets for clutter. We end up placing items there and then place yet more things on top of those items. They gather dust, and the clutter just ends up growing.

Start with the couch. Gather up any flotsam that may have washed up there. Loose clothing? Put it in the bedroom. Forgotten knitting projects? Set it aside. Remember that you're going to want to get in between the cushions eventually. Once you've cleared off the surface, pull out the cushions. You'll be surprised at what you find. Collect any loose change and throw out any gross food bits you find. You may want to consider breaking out the vacuum.

Turn your eye to other flat surfaces. See the coffee table? The odds are that it's accumulated its fair share of clutter, too. Take a moment to consider each item. Is it still imminently useful to your life? And does it bring you happiness? If the answer to either of those is "no," then pitch it in the donate pile.

Another item that tends to accumulate on coffee tables (and in stacks by the sides of the couch and shoved into bookshelves) are old magazines. The odds are that once you've read that magazine, you're not going to be reading it again. Why hang onto it? You can always donate it to your local library or just pitch it in the recycling bin.

Bookshelves

Speaking of literary items, take a look at that bookshelf of yours. Does it have anything crammed into it that isn't a book or a bookend? We tend to jam things every which way into the bookshelf and those things aren't always books. Pull everything out of your bookshelf. Survey all your reading material.The odds are that you have tomes hidden in there that you're never going to read again. A science textbook from college? Pitch it. A children's book in a house full of teenagers? Donate it.

Once you've winnowed your reading material, look at the other miscellaneous items you've pulled from the bookshelf. Go by the same rule: if you don't plan on using it in the foreseeable future, and it doesn't bring you joy, get rid of it.

Broken items

It's also likely that you've accumulated an array of broken items. Maybe they were shoved in between the bookshelf and the wall; maybe they were hiding under the couch. Either way, it's broken. If you're not handy, and you know that this item is beyond your capacity to repair, then why hang onto it? It's best to release it.

Sometimes we like to hang onto items because we think that we will be able to use a part of it to repair our other, working item. Or maybe we have the pipe dream that we'll take a class or learn the skill set necessary to repair it. Or perhaps we're waiting for a friend to come along who is conveniently handy enough to fix it. These are all pipe dreams. There's no reason to hang onto anything that doesn't work.

Tackle the rest of your drawers

You started out with one drawer, now finish it out my tackling the rest of them. We keep all kinds of things in our drawers, such as pens, stacks of paper, important documents, children's toys, office supplies, etc. But those items get easily jumbled and tossed around.

Take all of the drawer items out and put them in a pile. Sort them into items you actually use, and items that you never use. Once you've sorted them, further categorize the items that you intend to keep. Then, designate a drawer for each category of item. You may also want to use small Tupperware, baskets, or rubber bands to help keep the interior of your drawers neat.

Kitchen

The kitchen is where the sustenance you eat is made; therefore, it's important that this room is kept neat and sanitary. If you're constantly stressed by being surrounded by clutter, you're probably going to make poorer dietary choices for yourself.

Dishware

One of the easiest things to do is start with the dishes in your sink. Wash them all. Then, once they're clean, put them away. This immediately alleviates some of the clutter that is taking up space where it shouldn't be and makes the task slightly less daunting. Once your sink is clear, you can begin.

While on the subject of dishes, ask yourself if you have fancy dishware that you never use, but allegedly keep for "when company comes over." As someone who has owned this fancy dishware, I can attest that I never use it, even when company comes over. Donate it or sell it. The same could be said for your ever-increasing collection of coffee mugs. No one needs a coffee mug for every day of the month.

Flat surfaces

Just as with the living room, the flat surfaces in the kitchen are magnets for clutter. This includes counter tops, table tops, and chairs. Remove anything that doesn't belong in the kitchen and take it to its proper room. You can sort it out later in the other room, but for now, just get it out of the kitchen.

Once you've cleared off all your flat surfaces, begin sorting through your items into piles. Categorize them by items you actually use and/or that bring you happiness and items that do neither. Donate the items in the latter pile.

When you're sorting through your flat surfaces, odds are you're going to come across some cookbooks. In the day and age of the internet, most people are able to look up a recipe quickly. If you're someone who tends to look up recipes online rather than in a book, then owning a cookbook isn't going to do you much good. It's likely better to donate any cookbooks you have laying around. That said, if you have a cookbook that has sentimental value (such as being passed down through your family), or you're one of the rare breeds of people who actually peruse recipes written in print, then go ahead and keep a few. Donate the ones you don't use.

Utensils and cooking implements

We tend to collect kitchen utensils and other tools over time. Whether it's your fourth spatula, your third mixing bowl, or your second paring knife, some things have got to go. There's no reason to accumulate five baking sheets; unless you're running an underground bakery in your kitchen, no one is pumping out that amount of cookies.

Sort through your items. Choose the ones of the highest quality, and/or the ones that you use most often. If you have Pyrex mixing bowl that's been passed down to you by your grandmother, and thus has a great deal of sentimental value to you, then go ahead and hang onto it. There is a fine but definite line between ridding our home of excess stuff and depriving yourself of the items in your dwelling that bring real joy into your life.

One thing we all have too many of, though, is oven mitts. You may have accumulated a Smithsonian-worthy collection of these things over the years. No one needs ten pairs of oven mitts, so do yourself a favor and save the best ones and pitch the rest.

Refrigerator and pantry

Purging also includes food items. When was the last time you did a deep clean of your fridge or pantry? For many people, they only closely examine the contents of these places when they move into a new home. Expired items can lurk in refrigerator shelves for years at a time.

Start with one refrigerator or pantry shelf at a time. Check expiration dates. Throw out any food item that is past its freshness date. Of course, if it is in a recyclable container, then first empty out the food product into the trash, and then recycle the receptacle it was packaged in.

Do this until you've worked through all of the shelves of your fridge and pantry. Once the shelves are clear, give them a good scrubbing. If it's empty, you might as well give it a deep clean, right?

This serves two purposes. First, it eliminates health risk. Expired food can be a breeding ground for bacteria and put you at risk for food-borne illness. Secondly, it makes space in your fridge for food you will actually eat. This increases the efficiency of your refrigerator and pantry spaces.

You should also complete this process with your spice rack. The odds are that there is some oregano hiding back there from the last presidential administration. Keep only spices that you use with regularity and toss anything that is expired.

Kitchen gadgets

We've all been taken in by those 2 am infomercials advertising the latest kitchen gadget. Whether it's an egg cracker, a banana stand, or some other gizmo, most only get used once or twice before getting shoved into the back of a cabinet. Go through your gadgets and toss the dusty ones away.

Tupperware

There's probably a cabinet or shelf in your kitchen dedicated to a mountain of Tupperware. This is an especially problematic category of item to accumulate. The most frustrating part about putting away leftovers is the twenty-minute hunt for a container that has a matching lid.

Sort your containers and match lids to them as you go. Anything that doesn't have a lid or any lid that doesn't have a bottom should get donated or recycled. Once you have only matching sets, sort through them. Odds are you don't need nearly as many containers as you already have.

Under the sink

This is the place where most people keep their cleaning supplies. It's also a place that plastic bags commonly get shoved until it accumulates into a mass that takes up half the cabinet. If you're storing plastic bags here, or anywhere, do yourself a favor and cull majority of them. Many grocery stores have bins you can drop them at for recycling.

Cleaning supplies are also usually kept under the sink. While these are vital to keeping your space spic and span, check the labels. You've probably got some expired items lurking around under there. Also, purge anything that you haven't used in months and don't foresee yourself using anytime soon.

Junk Drawer

Finally, the junk drawer. Every house has one. It's the place we keep batteries, miscellaneous bits of string, and bread twist ties. Don't get me wrong, this drawer contains useful items, but it's also a cluttered nightmare.

Empty the drawer. Sort through all of the items. Throw out anything that is no longer functional like soy sauce packets or dead batteries. Now, put the items you want to keep back inside, using some organizational tricks like drawer dividers, rubber bands, or small baskets.

Bedrooms

The room where we retire at the end of the day should be an oasis of calm and serenity, allowing us to drift off into dreams. For many, though, the bedroom becomes a swamp of clothing and other paraphernalia. Oftentimes, the last thing people see before they fall asleep is a cluttered mess. To that end, let's break down the bedroom into five sections that need to be addressed. Closets and clothing will be addressed in the following section.

Bedside tables and flat surfaces

As previously stated, flat surfaces tend to accumulate items as time goes by. This includes bedside tables, cabinets, and the tops of dressers. Those items include old pairs of reading glasses, discarded books half-read before bed, magazines, or carelessly-tossed clothing.

Choose one surface and clear it off completely. Once the items are off, do a thorough scrubbing of the surface. After all, it's best to take advantage of the opportunity to do a deep cleaning. Just as you did before, separate out the items that are broken or otherwise useless.

Then, sort the items into those that you regularly use or that improve the quality of your life. Anything else can be put into the pile marked for donation, recycling, or the trash.

Under the bed

Aside from being the preferred hiding place of monsters, this space is also where dust bunnies congregate, as well as a whole host of forgotten items. Whether it fell down there, accidentally was shoved underneath, or was put there intentionally but then forgotten, you're never quite sure what you're going to find under the bed.

Clear out this space and sort the items as previously described. Do the deep-clean as previously described. Rather than putting items back here, try to see if there are other places you can store them. As a bonus fact, keeping the space under the bed clear of clutter is a helpful way to prevent bedbugs.

Extraneous Shoes

We tend to accumulate many different kinds of shoes throughout our lives; women are traditionally accused of being the worst perpetrators, but men can be guilty of this as well. Shoes can end up shoved in the closet, under the bed, or lurking in dusty, forgotten corners. To make the process easier, sort your shoes into categories such as sandals, dress shoes, winter shoes, and tennis shoes.

Keeping things seasonal is important. Just because it's the summer months and you're only wearing flipflops doesn't mean that you should pitch your winter boots. Conversely, if you're decluttering during the winter months, you shouldn't throw out all your sandals just because summer seems like a faraway dream.

Once you've winnowed away the ones that you haven't worn in the past year, you should devise a way to keep the shoes that you need readily available. Only keep those that you wear regularly. If you find yourself decluttering during the summer months, the odds are that you aren't wearing boots. Devise an organizational system to store away the off-season shoes. However, don't let the opportunity to put some shoes into storage trick you into keeping more than you need.

As a tip, you probably don't need more than three pairs of professional dress shoes. Most people only have one pair, but let's be generous in terms of matching for style. Similarly, you don't need more than one pair of tennis shoes. You can donate the rest.

Accessories

If you're someone who likes to wear a lot of accessories, they can stack up very fast. The problem with accessories is that the more outfits you accumulate, the more accessories you accumulate to pair with your outfits and clothing. These include accessories for hair, jewelry, scarves, and other such items.

It may be tempting to consider accessories as their own unique category and save them all in a box or in a cabinet. However, a majority of people simply do not need the sheer volume of accessories they collect. Unless you're a performer with a costume closet, there's no need for all of the frills we accumulate.

The odds are that your accessories are scattered about the room. As you're going from surface to surface and space to space cleaning, put accessories in their own pile. Once you've gone through the whole room and gathered them all together, you can now begin to sort.

You may want to consider keeping a few items if you give them a lot of mileage and/or they have a lot of sentimental value. But as you hold up each item and consider it individually, you will discover which ones you truly value, and which ones you can do without.

Unnecessary furniture

Once you've cleared off your spaces, it's time to take a look at the furniture you've gathered around your room. How much of it are you actually using, and how much of it was just holding belongings that you don't actually use? Once you've gotten rid of the items you don't use, these pieces of furniture will stick out like a sore thumb.

Some pieces of furniture, such as bedside tables and dressers, will be much emptier now that you've gone through the entire room. You can likely transfer items that you were storing in one place to another and consolidate our storage. This will leave certain pieces of furniture empty, which means that you can now consider getting rid of them.

Similarly, you may have a chair or table in your room that you've never actually sat on. Rather, it was covered in cast-off pieces of clothing and other miscellanea from your life. Once the clutter is gone, it will be obvious what pieces of furniture can be taken out of your room to give it a more open, airy feeling.

Clothing

While digging through your room, you'll probably discover a sweater you got for Christmas four years ago, but haven't worn since or a pair of pants you haven't fit into since high school. Clothing is one of the easiest items to accumulate, and that makes it one of the biggest challenges to declutter.

First and foremost, you'll want to make three piles. Those piles should be Keep, Donate, and Storage. Sorting through your clothing will be similar to sorting through your shoes, at least in that you will have to take into consideration that some of the items aren't going to be worn for another six months at least. Just because it's winter doesn't mean that you should throw out all of your shorts, and just because it's the middle of June doesn't mean you should purge your winter coat.

The Clothing you actually wear

It may help to sort your clothing into divisions of pants, shirts, socks, undergarments, sweatshirts, and whatever other categories of clothing you tend to wear. These categories will be different from person to person. A professional academic may have a huge array of blazers, while someone who works out at the gym may have a large amount of workout gear.

Take a moment to consider your lifestyle. What activities do you spend most of your time engaging in? You'll want to pay special attention during this phase, as this will help you determine the activities and beliefs that bring the most value to your life, which we will address in the next chapter. If you're an avid hiker, don't go overboard purging your outdoor clothing; if you spend the majority of your free time painting, you may want to keep a few of those paint-stained items that you wear while creating your art.

Off-season clothing

Once you've sorted your clothing into categories of things you wear with regularity and things you can let go, it's time to start dividing it up into what goes into your closet and what goes into storage. As we said in the section of shoes, don't allow the option of storage to become a trap where you keep more items than you actually need.

First, consider what season you are currently in. It is important to consider if you are in the middle of a season or are currently transitioning between seasons. This will affect which items you want to have readily available in your closet and which ones you can pack away into storage. If you're transitioning from spring into summer, you'll want to keep a few cold-weather items available, as it can still be chilly and rainy during this time. That said, it's probably safe to put all of your deep-winter gear into storage.

Coats

We have coats for every time of the year. We have heavy-duty winter coats, we have somewhat lighter coats for autumn, and we also have windbreakers for spring and when it rains. Generally, in summer, people tend to wear sweatshirts and hoodies. Keeping a range of coats is a good idea to keep you warm during the different seasons. However, keeping more than one or two in each category can cause your closet to overflow.

We all need a nice, heavy winter coat. That said, do you really need more than one? We can accumulate different winter coats throughout our lives, and instead of passing them on, we hoard them until there are no fewer than four sitting in the closet. Considering that most people only wear one, this is an awful waste of space. Also, taking into account the number of less fortunate people who don't have warm coats to wear during the winter, this is an excellent opportunity to donate the ones that you aren't wearing.

As you go through your coats, you'll probably notice that you have more than a few windbreakers or spring and autumn coats. Go through them and feel which ones you actually wear and which ones you really love. Odds are it'll only be one or two. Get rid of the rest and make some much-needed space in your closet. Go through the same process for sweatshirts and hoodies.

A note on clothing

In the 1940s, the average woman had nine different outfits. That number has skyrocketed today to be more than 30. Men tend to have fewer clothing options, but still, the numbers can add up. We've become so inundated with fast fashion that we accumulate huge amounts of clothing compared to less than a century ago.

This contributes to a process called decision fatigue. Every time we make a decision, it takes a toll on our brain and uses up a little bit of energy. Our society inundates us with choices on what to buy, what to watch, what to eat, and what to wear. You might think that more is better. But in this case, "more" ends up exhausting our brains so that we have a harder time applying our thought power to things that actually matter. Cutting down on the amount of clothing can help you simplify your decisions and lighten the mental load.

Another benefit is that as you go through your clothing, you'll realize which items you tend to wear more than others. When you realize the items that you give a lot of mileage, it'll give you a clearer picture of your own unique sense of style, which is another step towards a better understanding of yourself, your values, and your preferences.

Storage areas

Storage areas include that cabinet under the stairs, the garage, the basement, and the attic. Whatever space in your home you're using to keep items that won't fit elsewhere, things have probably accumulated in there over the years to the point of overwhelming you.

The process for going through your storage areas will be slightly different depending on your unique situation. If you have children or live in communal situations, such as with parents or roommates, then follow the instructions in the next paragraph. If you are a single person who does not live communally, skip the following paragraph and look at the one after it.

Living with others versus living solo

For those of you who live with multiple people, decluttering storage can be daunting. The easiest way to move forward is to create piles for each individual living in the household. If you have children, you can create piles for them. If you are living with other people, you can have them join you in the decluttering process and make a communal activity out of it. Each adult person can sort through their respective piles and decide to label them as Keep or Donate. This can be a great bonding experience.

If you live alone, then on the bright side, your pile of stuff is likely going to be much smaller. On the downside, you're going to have to do all the work by yourself. Categorize your items as you go; try to keep the number of piles limited, but also don't be afraid to add your categories when you really need them. These categories can include tools, furniture, gardening equipment, memorabilia, etc. Once you've set your categories, you can move forward onto the next steps.

Tools

It's good to keep a hammer and nails around if you need them. Likewise, keeping a screwdriver is always a good idea. If you're not very handy, though, then there's no reason for you to keep a hold of a large buzz saw. If you don't perform your own home repairs or you aren't particularly handy, then you probably don't need large power tools

If you *are* handy, though, and carpentry is one of your hobbies, then, by all means, keep your tools. But if you have tools that you haven't used in more than six months, it may be worthwhile to consider whether or not you really need them after all. Keeping a basic tool kit readily available is always a good idea, and perhaps, that toolkit shouldn't be buried in the back of the garage.

Furniture

When we buy new furniture, sometimes, we move our old furniture into the basement. Or we temporarily move it out of the room, but then realize we like the room better without that table or armchair. So, the piece of furniture stays in storage but never gets removed from the home. Furniture is large and bulky and can easily eat up your valuable storage space.

If you've removed a piece of furniture from a particular room and found you liked it better that way, ask yourself: do you really need this piece of furniture in the first place? If it's a treasured family heirloom, but it's just gathering dust in the attic, you may want to consider passing it along to another family member who can proudly display the item. If you're holding onto it because it's a valuable antique, then try to sell it. Either way, get it gone.

Gardening and yard work tools

This section will only apply to those who have an outdoor space to maintain or a garden to upkeep. If you live in a condo or apartment without any yard, you can skip ahead to the next portion. However, if you do have a lawn you have to keep mowed or a garden you have to tend, then this section is for you.

There are many tools that are useful in the upkeep of the exterior of your home. As you sort through your tools, reflect on how often you use each one. Do you have a hedge clipper, but no hedges? If you have redundant tools, don't' be afraid to let them go.

Similarly, if you have amassed gardening tools throughout the years, but have never gotten around to actually starting your garden, it may be time to reevaluate whether or not you keep those tools. This is an excellent opportunity to really examine how you spend your time and if you truly think you can scrape up the hours necessary in your busy life to commit to tending a garden. This is an example of the self-reflection that minimalism can bring to your life.

If you don't have space in your life for the project that the tool is meant for, then let the tool go.

Memorabilia

As you go through the storage area, it's likely that you'll come across memorabilia from your childhood, from loved ones, or from significant moments in your life. These can be among the trickiest items to categorize and sort through because they will often have a huge amount of sentimental value.

The key to sorting through family memorabilia is to identify the key memories and people that the objects represent. Do you have other objects that represent the memory or person that you're holding onto? Which items are truly close to your heart? There is a difference between items that have true value to you and a reluctance to throw away any object at all that reminds you of someone you love or a treasured memory.

It is also helpful, on a philosophical level, to realize the difference between the objects and the memory. The memory is something that will always be with you; an object is just a physical anchor for the memory. Realize the value of the memory over the physical "stuff" will help you reevaluate your priorities.

A note on "just in case"

One of the biggest reasons we hold onto stuff we don't use is if we need it "just in case." What if we need that ten-year-old fire extinguisher? What if we need that old cabinet in case one of our breaks? What if we need to use the broken vacuum cleaner for replacement parts for the one that works?

"Just in case" is a hole we fall into that traps us in clutter. A good rule of thumb is the 20/20 rule. If the thing you're considering keeping can be replaced in less than twenty minutes for less than twenty dollars, then it's not worth the amount of space it's taking up in your home. The mentality of scarcity and lack is one of the primary reasons that unwanted belongings pile up in our home. When we go through our parent's attic, oftentimes, we ask ourselves, "why on earth did they hold onto this?" Well, when your children or friends go through your storage space, odds are they're going to ask themselves the same questions.

A note on sentimental items

There is a difference between making room in your life for those things you truly value and living like a monk in a prison-like cell bereft of any adornment. There is no reason to deprive yourself of the joys and comforts of items that you truly love. If you have a locket that your grandmother gave you, then there's no reason to get rid of it. When you compare that locket to the ten other necklaces that you picked up at some fast fashion shop, though, it should be clear what needs to stay and what needs to go.

Having items you love isn't a bad thing. Minimalism is about getting rid of the piles and piles of unneeded items so that you can discover which items have real meaning for you. When you are surrounded only by items that are imminently useful or that bring obvious happiness to your life, then you will be more open to happiness from other areas of your life as well.

Things to keep in mind

On a purely logistical note, there will be times when you're tempted to add a "maybe" pile as you're categorizing your items. It can be difficult to decide at the moment whether or not you really want to get rid of an item, so you put off deciding until later. I'll tell you right now, don't do it.

Eventually, you'll find the "maybe" pile getting bigger and bigger as you sit on the fence. All you're doing is giving into your own indecision and making a bigger problem for yourself to solve later. The idea with decluttering is to simplify your life, but a "maybe" pile will only complicate the process and give you yet another task to stress out about later. Do yourself a favor and make the hard decisions at the moment. Your future self will thank you.

Be ruthless. It can be easy to fall into the hole of indecision. Use your gut when you're going through your items. Your snap judgments are in touch with your subconscious and will give you the best indication as to whether or not an item is truly useful or truly brings you happiness. Being ruthless can be difficult, but it will get easier as you go along. Trust your gut; it will simplify the process.

Chapter 5: How to Declutter Your Mind

Minimalism is a philosophy that extends to every area of your life, not just your home. The same idea extends from getting rid of physical items to simplifying your mind. The mind can be full of anxious thoughts constantly running. It's rare that any of us gets a true moment of silence in our minds. Our minds are noisy for many of the same reasons that our homes are full of clutter. We live in a society that is constantly designed to fill our minds with chatter and to fill our spaces with belongings. The news cycle is on twenty-four hours, there are advertisements wherever you go, and technology is constantly pinging us with notifications. Finding a moment of mental silence can be a miraculous feat. This chapter, though, will show you how to pull it off.

Move past the past

There are many reasons that our minds become cluttered. A wise man once said that those who have anxiety are living in the future, and those who have depression are living in the past. Both of these problems stem from not being in touch with the present. Many people become haunted by their pasts; their histories are like ghosts that rattle chains in their mind, never letting them rest or be at peace.

There is a whole slew of things that can cause a person to become locked in their past. Traumatic events can anchor a person to a certain point in their history or development so that they never emotionally mature beyond that point. Coping mechanisms that we pick up during difficult or challenging times can hold us back from moving forward. This section will outline some of the reasons that people become locked in the past, as well as how to let go, heal, and live in the present.

Replaying old conversations

One of the pieces of mental clutter that take up the most space is the replaying of old conversations in our heads. How many times have you lain awake at night, obsessively going over verbal exchanges that happened not days or weeks, but years ago? We get fixated on old conversations where we did not communicate clearly or where we think we made fools of ourselves. Or, we replay conversations where we wish we had said something differently, or reimagine saying the perfect retort during an argument.

This is one of the most nefarious forms of mental clutter. First and foremost, it anchors us to the past so that we cannot focus on the present. Another troubling aspect of this behavior is that it usually happens at night when we are lying in bed. We should be drifting off peacefully to sleep; instead, our minds are spinning at full speed. A time for relaxation is instead a time for stress and anxiety. Is it any wonder that, as a society, we don't get enough sleep or that the sleep we get is of poor quality?

Old hang-ups

We all have arguments that we've been in over the years. Whether a disagreement with a loved one or that inconsiderate person who cut you off in traffic, we tend to hang onto grudges. Worse, not only do we hang onto them, but we replay them in our mind or bring them up in conversation. Small aggressions done to them are something that people can hang onto for their entire lives. However, the person who was rude to you in the supermarket or the person who cut you off in traffic has probably forgotten that moment entirely. If they have forgotten it, then why are you still holding onto that moment? The person who angered you is free and unburdened; you should allow yourself that gift as well.

Previous relationships

Another thing that can cause us to get stuck in the past is old relationships. For whatever reasons, sometimes, love doesn't work out, friendships end, and sometimes, even family members fade out of our lives. When connections that we invest in emotionally come to an end, it can be an extremely painful experience. However, eventually, time will heal wounds into mere scars, which will fade as the years pass. But those wounds will not heal if we are constantly picking the scabs by indulging in poor mental habits around this kind of pain.

It is all right to grieve when people leave your life. Sometimes, things come up that remind us of them, and we get sad. This is completely normal and healthy. What is unhealthy is when you spend hours nit-picking the relationship trying to assign blame or thinking of what you could have done differently to make the person stay. Don't get me wrong, it's important to get closure on relationships; this is a process that needs to be approached mindfully and intentionally, perhaps with the help of a licensed professional. Wallowing in a lost connection is the opposite, and will only cause you to get mired in the past.

Traumas

This is perhaps the trickiest mental hole we can fall into. Traumas are very real and can lead to diagnosable disorders and chemical imbalances in the brain, such as Clinical Depression or Post-Traumatic Stress Disorder. Telling someone to "just get over" trauma is unwise, and potentially even so damaging as to compound the original trauma.

That said, trauma takes up a huge amount of space in our mind, though many people don't realize it because it is so repressed. Many damaging and destructive thought patterns and behavioral patterns stem from the trauma that can further clutter up our mental space.

If you are someone who has experienced trauma, then beginning to address that trauma is the key to your mental decluttering. All of the other things mentioned in this chapter are merely window dressings when compared to our deepest, darkest shadows.

Just like decluttering your home is an intense, tiring, and ongoing process, decluttering your mind is as well. It is a lifestyle decision, a lifelong commitment, and an ongoing process. The ways that people choose to address their trauma are highly individual, but some of the most successful people choose methods such as talk therapy, deepening their spiritual connection, journaling, or taking up a meditation practice.

Letting go

Despite how easy a certain Disney princess made it seem, it's harder to move past something than simply singing "let it go." Despite this, the benefits are very real. If you consciously choose to begin to move past the things that are anchoring to your past, you will be able to breathe more freely and experience a much less frantic mind.

If you find yourself experiencing difficulty with this process, it may be advisable to enlist the help of a psychological professional, trusted member of the clergy, or other trained and trusted person to guide you through the process. A brief process for allowing yourself to engage in this is outlined below.

Each time an old hang-up, past conversation, or other pieces of mental clutter arises, do the following:

- Take a deep breath in. Exhale slowly
- Hold the moment firmly in your mind.
- Observe the emotions swirling around the memory.
- Do not judge the emotions, merely observe them.
- Once you have observed the emotions, state the following:
    - I forgive myself for holding onto this memory.
    - I forgive myself for how I acted in this situation.
    - I do not need to hold onto this. It no longer serves me.
    - I release my attachment to this memory.

Repeat the last line slowly, as many times as you need to. As a side note, the same memory or pain may come up multiple times. You may have to go through this process several times with the same memory. However, engaging with this process is like working out a muscle. The more you do it over time, the stronger you become. And in the end, the more peaceful your mind will be.

Come back from the future

We've discussed people being anchored in the mud of their past. However, people can also cast their consciousness into tomorrow or events that have not yet come to pass. Having their attention always focused on some distant day prevents them from living in the moment as surely as being stuck in the past does. If they're always worried about the future, then those worries are constantly racing through their mind, taking up valuable space, time, and attention.

Anxiety

The textbook definition of this word involves feelings of worry, nervousness, or unease. Anxiety brings with it a frenetic quality to the mind and tenseness to the body. The physical effects of this increased level of tenseness and stress are higher levels of stress hormones in the system. These increased level of stress hormone cause an increased risk for cardiovascular disease, high blood pressure, heart attack, stroke, a compromised immune system, and insomnia.

Short-term effects of high stress on the body include headaches, upset stomach, lethargy, and loss of libido. Whether in the short-term or the long-term, spending too much time obsessing or worrying about the future is terrible for our health. Reigning in these neurotic tendencies is vital for healthy mental hygiene.

Fear of the unknown

One of the main reasons that we have anxieties in the first place is due to our fear of the unknown. Until someone invents a time machine, we can never be one hundred percent certain what the future holds. That is just a fact we have to make peace with; worrying about it only makes us sicker.

This fear of the unknown is one of the biggest drivers behind our packrat tendencies. We don't know if the day will come that we will need an item, so we save it "just in case." However, that "just in case" day rarely comes, if ever. And you're left with more physical items cluttering up your home and more nonsensical worries cluttering up your mind.

The process of decluttering your physical space will often force you to address this fear of the unknown. It may also help you come to peace with the uncertainty of the future.

Fear of lack

Another habit of poor mental hygiene is the tendency to fear lack. Our society has drilled into us that in order to be happy, we have to be successful. In order to appear successful, we need to own certain things. If we don't own those things, then we will be neither happy nor successful. Our society has also drilled into us that not having those things is one of the worst fates someone can suffer; to be labeled as "poor" or to be impoverished is the worst fate one could imagine. So we hoard physical belongings in an attempt to stave off this fate.

Logically, we must come to terms with the fact that this is a lie that our culture has sold us. People all over the world have found happiness in many different circumstances, many who don't own anything at all. However, knowing mentally that this is a lie and trying to decondition ourselves to this lie are two very different tasks. The act of decluttering may test you in this regard, but it is also a great opportunity to deprogram yourself to this untruth.

Scarcity mentality

When we live in fear of not owning anything, we become locked into what can be called a "scarcity mentality." The trademarks of the scarcity mentality are constant mental worrying about not having enough of something, whether it's vacation days, money, or toilet paper. Don't get me wrong: if you're experiencing food or housing instability, then some level of worry is completely normal.

For a majority of other people though, they don't realize just how good they have it. If you have a stable roof over your head, food in your fridge, working heat, and an incoming paycheck, then you are vastly better off than the majority of the world's population. The fact is that the brain tends to focus on the things we *don't* have, rather than appreciating the things that we do have.

Decluttering can help you to learn to truly appreciate the items you choose to keep and can help you develop a mentality of gratitude rather than scarcity.

It feels good to worry

One of the reasons that the human brain falls into the worry trap is simply a matter of neurochemistry. When we're being productive and crossing things off of our lists, our brain releases endorphins to make us feel good. And though it may seem counterintuitive, the brain also releases endorphins when we worry.

The brain releases endorphins when we worry because the brain still feels like we're productive, even if we're just sitting on the couch. So our reward center gets activated, and it feels good to worry, even if we spend all afternoon staring at the wall and don't actually get anything done.

The release of endorphins is one of the sneakiest and problematic issues with decluttering your mind— because our brain gets a chemical reward even if we don't get anything done. The trick is to resist the temptation and reject the false reward your brain gives you when you worry.

When we live in the future instead of the present, we miss out on our lives. We spend years and years of our lives climbing all of the ladders society tells us to climb. We work hard at some company selling insurance. We get the promotion and the raise. We buy a new car, then a house with a white picket fence, then a dog. And then we have children and have to buy nice things for them, too. Until suddenly you wake up and realize you're 45 and that the ladder you've climbed was against the wrong wall—and then all your alleged happiness goes up in smoke. This unfortunate journey is behind many a midlife crisis.

We think for so long that once we get a certain thing, we'll be happy. Until the day comes that we arrive at that thing and we find we aren't happy at all. So, then, the trick must be to find happiness wherever we are—because it isn't anywhere else.

Everything else is just an illusion taking up valuable space in our minds, clouding us from enjoying the present moment.

Focus on the present

There are many mental traps that we can get stuck in. We can become hung up on the past, unable to move on from things that have happened to us. We can project our mind into the future, inventing problems that don't even exist. Unfortunately, it is very easy for the human mind to fall victim to these fates. However, you don't have to suffer this fate. You can deliberately choose to free yourself from these prisons, to remove these cobwebs and lies from your brain, and experience a mind that is at peace.

Discover your body

When our minds are constantly firing, all of our focus is on our head. We don't notice when our bodies are sending us signals. We've all heard the story of someone who's been so engrossed in work that they forget to eat, sleep, or go to the bathroom. While this is an extreme case, to a lesser degree, we all suffer from it.

How often have you been rushing frantically around and develop a whopper of a headache? Only later do you realize that you are severely dehydrated, but your mind was so preoccupied with multitasking that you didn't pay attention to your growing thirst. It's like when you have the radio playing so loudly in your car that you don't hear the funny noise it's starting to make and only realizing something is wrong when smoke starts to pour out from under the hood.

Utilizing techniques to quiet your mind allows you to get in tune with your body. You'll be astounded at all of the small signals you're able to hear when you turn down your frenetic mental radio. This will also help you achieve better health, as you begin to understand your body's needs better.

Get in touch with your mind

It's astounding how many people out there fear their own mind. They're deathly afraid that if they slow down enough to hear their own thoughts, they will drown in their trauma. Or they have been so immersed in the cultural paradigm of fear surrounding stillness and quiet that they avoid it at all costs.

Taking the time to understand the nature of your own mind is a wonderful opportunity. There is a reason that Zen masters are so happy. Learning to appreciate the stillness in your mind is like learning to appreciate your decluttered home. Whereas, before there were chaos and disarray, now there is enough space and stillness to be able to breathe; you can appreciate the way sunlight comes through the window and lights up your home. Similarly, when you declutter your mind, you can learn to appreciate joy as it comes through your life and lights up your heart like sunlight coming through a window.

A renewed love of life

When we are children, every experience is new. We have awe and joy at everything we see and are genuinely excited to wake up in the morning and experience the world. As we age, we lose touch with this spirit. Instead, we fall into thought patterns of cynicism and depression, forgetting the joy with which we once experienced our lives.

When you declutter your mind, you also set to work clearing out destructive and negative mental habits and thought patterns. Once you sweep out the cynicism and regret, you have room to live your life again truly. You're able to rediscover your childlike wonder and fall in love with the world once more. But you can only accomplish this if you set about the work of tidying up your mind.

Discover your true values

One of the most important methods of decluttering your mind is to discover those things which are most important to you. Only when you truly understand what you care about most are you able to clean house in your mind and make space for those treasured things in your life. There are many ways to figure out what you value in life, though this section will only cover five of them: journaling, self-reflection, retreat, vision boards, and talk therapy.

Journaling

Keeping a written record of your days is a great way to begin to get a birds-eye view of the patterns of your life. Plus, committing the events of the day and your feelings about them to paper forces you to process them and think about them. Being able to think critically about the events in your life gives you a deeper understanding of how you feel about things and how the challenges you experience affect you.

When you write things down, you understand better what brings you joy in life, and what brings you pain. You also are able to comprehend how you behave and think in certain situations. This is a wonderful chance for self-examination to help you discover things in your life that may need to change, as well as to find out what things matter most to you.

Self-reflection

Another method of discovering your true values is to set aside time for reflection simply. While journaling involves committing your thoughts to write, self-reflection can be as simple as making time in your day to mentally sort through the things happening in your life.

Making time to sit on the back porch with a cup of coffee is one of the greatest gifts you could give to yourself. Not only does it give you the chance to enjoy the stillness and take pleasure in the little moments, but it also gives you the chance to do in your own mind what journaling helps you to do in writing.

As you sort through the events of your life, notice your feelings about things as they arise. Pay particular attention to the things that make you happiest and fill you with joy. Try devoting more time and space in your life to those areas.

Retreat

Sometimes, our lives are so hectic and busy that we are unable to think clearly. For some people, the stress is so great that the only way they're able to gain any kind of clarity is to physically remove themselves from their lives for a period of time. While this is not a practical option for many, for those who can afford it, spending a period of time in retreat can do wonders for their mental health.

When you decide to remove yourself from your life for a while, don't go somewhere that's loud and busy like a big city or ski resort. Choose a place like a mountain cabin or a quiet apartment near the beach. Spend time in nature in a place where your vision can stretch out to the horizon. Then your mind can stretch out and attend to the question: what do you want most out of life?

Vision boards

Some people are verbally inclined; for them, writing things down can help them mentally map them out, as well as process them. For those that operate on a more visual level, a vision board can help them engage with this same process. Vision boards work by forcing you to spend time thinking about what you wish for most in your life. These don't have to be in words but can be in the form of feelings or impressions in your mind.

Once you have these things in your mind, go out and hunt down images that capture what you truly desire. You can clip from magazines, cut up old posters, or print pictures from online. Once you've gathered your pictures, attach them to a vision board, and hang that board up somewhere, you will see it every day. A vision board can serve as a physical, daily reminder of what you truly value in your life.

Therapy

For those that have difficulty accessing the depths of their own mind, it can seem beyond hopeless to try and figure out what they truly want out of life. If you've tried the above methods but not made any progress, enlisting outside help can be a great benefit. There can be a lot of cultural stigma around therapy, but there shouldn't be.

Getting an outside perspective can help you see your life much more clearly. Not to mention, a professional will be able to equip you with tricks and tools above and beyond those mentioned within the pages of this book.

Cultivating mindfulness

So, you've done the work and discovered your true values. Now, how do you train your mind so that you can give yourself the ability to live a life in accordance with those values? In order to do this, you have to be able to be in touch with the present moment. To be in touch with the present moment, you have to cultivate mindfulness. This section will provide you with advice, as well as a few methods, to cultivate mindfulness.

Stop multitasking

The first piece of advice I have for you is to stop multitasking. In this day and age, we think that we can stack tasks in order to be more productive. When you multitask, though, this just isn't true. The truth is, you can either do one thing well or two things poorly. The choice is yours.

Dividing your attention between multiple tasks prevents you from being fully present at the moment. Instead, your mind is frantically skipping back and forth between them, and the end results are poorer. You will find yourself much calmer if you allow yourself to simply do one thing at a time.

Slow down

This fast-paced world has tricked us into thinking that in order to be happy, we have to be productive and that in order to be productive, we have to fill every waking moment of every day with activity. This mentality has infected us to the point that many of us feel guilty for simply taking a day off.

When you are attending to a chore or are driving during your commute, etc., refocus your attention and slow down. Do whatever you are doing carefully and deliberately, with your full attention. Giving your full attention to the task at hand will anchor you in the present moment and momentarily dispel all mental clutter.

Breathe

We hear this piece of advice all the time. But how many of us really do it? How often do you take a moment to remove yourself from a situation, step outside, and get a sweet lungful of fresh air? I'll bet it's been quite a while.

Whenever you remember, stop whatever you're doing, and allow yourself to take several deep breaths. Start from your lower belly and inhale all the way up through your lungs. Once you've taken a nice long inhale, exhale slowly and deliberately. Do this at least three times, though more is better.

Conscious breathing anchors you in your physical body and quiets the mind. This is another excellent tool that quiets the thoughts and helps you to cultivate a clutter-free mind.

Be where you are

This may seem laughably simple. After all, you're only able to be in one place a time—how could you possibly be anywhere else? Well, this one refers to your mind. When you cast your mind out to worry about the future or let yourself wallow in some aspect of your past, you aren't present.

Whenever you catch yourself doing this, take a moment to recall your mind. As you do this, though, it's important to gently bring the mind back, without anger or judgment. If you're constantly berating yourself, then you're going to associate mental decluttering with feeling bad and cultivate anger towards yourself. This is the opposite of what minimalism hopes to achieve.

5-4-3-2-1

When you find yourself not being present or notice that you are getting really worked up, you can use the 5-4-3-2-1 method to anchor yourself back in the present moment.

- Look for **5** things you can **see**.

- Identify **4** things you can **touch**
- Find **3** things you can **hear**
- Discover **2** things you can **smell**
- Look for **1** thing you can **taste**

This method was originally developed to help people who suffer from anxiety. However, it is an excellent tool that anyone can use to anchor a wandering mind firmly back into the present moment. The senses are physical links between the present moment and the brain.

Do something you love every day

One of the reasons that we don't want to spend time in the present moment is because, oftentimes, the present moment is hard. Why let your consciousness be anchored in the harsh reality of today when it can dream about a more pleasant tomorrow or a happy memory?

In order to declutter your mind, you have to be able to stay in the present moment. In order to stay in the present moment, you have to want to do it. In order to want to do it, you need to find reasons to stay anchored here. So, how do you do that?

Make time every day to do something that you enjoy. If there is one small thing that gives you happiness every single day, then you'll be better able to appreciate today, instead of living in yesterday or tomorrow.

Set intentions

The goal of decluttering your mind is to allow you to fully live in the present moment, to find mental peace and quiet, and to be able to apply your brain power to the things that really matter. What are the things that really matter, though? And how do you learn to pay attention to them? In the past sections, we've explored how to discover your core values, and this section will explore how to apply those values. The way to apply those core values to your life is the process of setting intentions.

Intentions are defined as an aim, plan, purpose, or objective. To set intentions, you need to examine your core values and make a few concrete plans to apply them to your life. For example, if you determined that family connection was one of the most important criteria for your happiness, then the intention you set may look like "I am going to see my far-away family at least twice a year during the holidays and my local family members at least once a month." If you determine that your physical health is one of the most important things to you, then the intention you set may sound like "I am going to cut my refined sugar intake in half and go running at least three times a week." Core values are important but vague. Intentions are the concrete plans you make to align your life with those values.

The unintentional life

There is a unique sort of tragedy to someone who lives without making any waves, "going with the flow" until they wake up on their death bed and realizing that they sleepwalked through their life. This type of person usually doesn't have a clear idea of what they want for themselves and typically follows the society script: get a high-status job, get married, buy a house, have kids, go on a few vacations a year, and finally, be able to be happy for a few years once they retire.

This is the kind of life that births the mid-life crisis: when someone suddenly wakes up, realizes their time in this world is already half-over, and that they haven't let themselves enjoy very much of it. This is also the ideal consumer for all of the incessant, blaring advertising that is constantly directed at us. The best driver of a company's profits is someone who mindlessly consumes the latest product, dutifully following the societal script dictating what they need to purchase in order to be happy.

Record your intentions

The first step is to examine your core values and then to extrapolate concrete plans based off of those values, as is described earlier on in this section. Once you've settled on an intention though, the work doesn't end. Just thinking about doing something won't actually cause you to do it; sometimes, we need a bit of "oomph" to muster the will power to accomplish our goals.

Once you've created your intentions, whether it's being kinder to people or simply eating more fruit, you need to record it. Writing it down is one of the best ways to bring it physically into the world. Plus, the act of writing it down, ingrains it into your neural pathways. But you don't need to stop there.

To take it one step further, write your intention down, and then put it in a place where you will look at it every single day. Put it on a piece of paper and then attach that piece of paper to your bathroom mirror, so that you see it first thing in the morning. You can also put it in places that you spend a lot of time, such as on a sticky note attached to your computer monitor or on your dashboard next to your steering wheel. Having your intentions written out in multiple places is immensely helpful, because once you see it; you are able to empty your mind of whatever trivial thing was taking up your mental space. You can clear out the memory of that jerk who cut you off in traffic or the fast food worker who got your order wrong, and you can focus back in on the things that really matter.

Course-correcting

Repetition is the key. The more often you see your written-down intentions, the more often you will be reminded. The more often you are reminded, the easier it is to course-correct when you find yourself slipping. Just like with anything, getting started is the hardest part. Most people will struggle in the beginning as they adjust to these new mental habits. Written intentions can be a great help.

Having written reminders is like having a safety net under you as you walk a tightrope. Just like with learning to walk a tightrope, you're going to fall fairly often. But having a written reminder of what you hope to accomplish will allow you to stand up, dust yourself off, climb back up, and keep on trying. Eventually, you will master this skill! But you may mess up a bit at the beginning—which is totally normal.

Meditation

Perhaps, the practice that most often comes to mind when people think about mastering their thoughts is the practice of meditation. This is an ancient method that is used by groups all over the world, though it is most often associated with Buddhism and Hinduism. Despite these associations, meditation can be learned in ways that are completely secular and don't require any specific kind of spiritual belief. The textbook definition is to focus your mind for some period of time, either in stillness or with the aid of some kind of repetitious, spoken mantra. It has many benefits, including improved levels of focus, relaxation, and less cluttered thoughts.

How does meditation help?

Meditation doesn't just give you intangible benefits. There are very real, measurable effects on the body and brain. People who meditate have higher levels of theta (relaxation) brain waves, as well as lowered levels of stress hormones such as cortisol in their bloodstream.

On a more psychological note, meditation gives us the opportunity to see just how truly noisy are minds are. It's only when we slow down, and sit quietly, that we are truly able to observe the constant stream of brain chatter and mental clutter. By paying attention to these levels of noise, we can begin to tame them and turn down our mental "volume knob."

By dedicating ourselves to a regular meditation practice, we can flex our mental muscles and develop the discipline to create the peace and quiet we crave. Aside from having a more peaceful mind, you will also observe an increased ability to focus on the task at hand, lowered levels of anxiety, and the ability to stay grounded in the present moment.

Creating the space

First, you'll want to create a space that is empty of distractions. Mute your phone and leave it in the other room. Turn off the television. Close the windows if you live in a noisy neighborhood. Ensure that nobody is going to be walking through your home and distracting you.

Many pictures depict people sitting on the floor folded into pretzels. There is no need to sit this way if you are physically unable. You'll want to sit upright, perhaps on a cushion on the floor or a straight-backed chair. Avoid sitting on the couch or other surfaces that is too comfortable—you may wind up falling asleep.

Watch the breath

Next, you'll want to watch your breath. The most common way to do this is to inhale and exhale slowly. After you finish each exhale, count your breath. Once you reach ten, start over at "one." The cyclical nature of this counting gives the brain something to do. We all have something that meditation masters call "monkey mind," that is constantly chattering like a monkey. Counting your breaths gives this part of your brain something to do so that it isn't constantly running its mouth.

Watch the body

As your mind quiets itself, anchor yourself in your body. This grounds you firmly in the present moment and is also a great opportunity to reconnect with your physical form. Many people spend so much of their day in their heads that they lose touch with their body.

As you breathe deeply, you can start to scan your body. Start from the tips of your toes and slowly work your way up. Notice anything that is painful, any creaky joints or tight muscles. Once you work your way all the way up to the top of your head, return to counting your breaths. You can use this insight later to speak with a doctor or create an exercise regimen.

Thoughts like clouds

As you count your breaths, thoughts are going to arise. The trick, though, is to not attach your attention to them. Treat your thoughts like clouds. They form out of nothing, drift, and then disappear. They drift across the sky of your mind, and you are like a child lying on a grassy hill watching them go by.

Keep focusing on your breath, and let the thoughts come and go. They aren't important. Once you move your attention away from your thoughts, those thoughts lose their power over you.

Don't be too hard on yourself

There are going to be times when a real dose of thought comes along, and it distracts you away from scanning your body or counting your breaths. When this happens, don't be too hard on yourself. Everyone has challenges in the beginning. Plus, berating yourself doesn't help you meditate any better; it actually makes meditating harder.

Instead, when you notice that your attention has wandered, gently redirect your attention back to your breath. There isn't a single person learning to meditate who has a perfectly thought-free mind. So, when you get distracted, as everyone does, don't be too hard on yourself. It is a very normal part of the learning process.

Exercise

Though it may seem counter-intuitive, another great way to declutter your mind is to exercise your physical body. Why is that? When we don't move our body, we can have a lot of pent-up energy that doesn't get released. This energy works its way up to our brain, where it can manifest as anxiety, neuroses, anger, or ceaseless chatter. Therefore, by releasing this excess energy from the body, we are preventing it from infiltrating our mind.

Physical benefits

There are a million scientific studies out there that extol the virtues of exercise and its long-term health benefits, so I won't go into those right now. Exercise is also well-known to release endorphins into the bloodstream, which can elevate mood, and sometimes, even give off feelings of euphoria. These mood-elevation benefits allow you to more fully enjoy your life and be more anchored in the present moment.

On the flip side, a lack of physical exercise has also been definitively linked to worse mental health. Inactivity co-occurs with many mental illnesses. While it is dangerous to link the two and correlation does not equal causation, if you are able to exercise, then your mental health is likely better off than people who don't.

Get more in touch with your body

As stated in the section on meditation, many people spend their lives in their heads and treat their bodies as a vehicle that gets their heads to and from various places. Living solely in your head not only makes you more likely to get stuck in the future or the past, but it also leads to a dangerous disconnect from your body.

When you aren't anchored in your physical body, you aren't paying attention to its warning signs. A metaphor could be that instead of seeing the gas light go on in your car, you're so preoccupied that suddenly you roll to a stop and aren't able to continue on. How often do we forget to drink water? Or eat?

Being more in touch with your physical body not only anchors you in the present moment but also lets you learn your body's rhythms and what is "normal" and "abnormal." This can be a great boon when you realize something is wrong and are able to get to the doctor for early or preventative treatment.

Plus, your body will be stronger! Someone who gets winded walking up a flight of stairs will revel in the wonder at being able to run a marathon after diligent training. Being in better shape lets you feel powerful and strong, and your body will be better able to stand up to the trials and tribulations of aging.

Chapter 6: How to Declutter Your Life

So far, we've talked about how to declutter your house and how to declutter your mind. Let's go one step farther and expand these methods to discuss how you can use the philosophy of minimalism to declutter your life. Many of us feel the time crunch; how often have you heard the phrase "I wish there were more hours in the day"? Well, there aren't ever going to be more hours in the day—so we have to make the hours we do have count. To make those hours count, we have to assess how we spend our time and redirect our focus and time into those things that represent our core values.

Toxic relationships

One of the most important things in our lives are our connections to the people we love. However, sometimes, the people we love aren't good for us. Some relationships are damaging; these are called "toxic relationships." A relationship of this kind is characterized by behaviors of the toxic person that are mentally, emotionally, or physically damaging to the other person. A relationship of this kind will leave you feeling drained, sad, anxious, and exhausted. Toxic people may tear others down and be needlessly cruel. These are the easiest kind to spot.

The harder kind to spot are those friends that are caught in self-destructive behaviors and constantly require your time and attention to the console or help them; this kind of relationship can be exhausting, and while you may feel like you are taking a nurturing role, the truth is that you are acting as an enabler. Both of these kinds of relationships are damaging in their own way.

Healthy relationships leave you feeling supported and loved. There may be some criticism, but it is given in the spirit of self-improvement and to call out problematic behaviors, rather than for the sake of meanness. Solid relationships are based on mutual trust and respect and should never leave you feeling mentally, emotionally, or physically drained or abused.

Why we hang onto toxic relationships

If these relationships are so bad for us, then why do we hang onto them? We hold on precisely because the connection to loved ones is so important to us. When we love someone, we don't want to let them go, whether it's a long-time friend, a romantic partner, or a family member.

We may say, "Well, I've known them for my whole life! I can't cut them out!" or "This person is family, so I have a duty to stand by them." If we have low self-esteem, we may think "Even if this person makes me feel very sad, I don't know if anyone else will ever fall in love with me" or "I'm so bad at making friends that if I lose this one, I'll be alone." The first kind of reasoning is based on delusion. The second kind is based on low self-esteem.

Friendships

It can be hard to let go of friendships, especially when we have known them for decades or since childhood. We cultivate relationships with our peers at school, at work, or at extracurricular activities. These people become a kind of adopted family, and you form bonds based on shared opinions and interests. Good friends make life much more pleasant and fun.

One of the things that make moving to a new city so scary is the fact that we know we'll have to make new friends. The sense of isolation and loneliness that comes from being alone is terrible. So, it would make sense that we would want to hang onto every single friend we have, especially if we don't have many, to begin with.

It is useful to take note of how you feel after spending time with your friends. Do you feel happy, invigorated, and satisfied? Or do you feel exhausted, drained, and sad? Don't get me wrong, there's a difference between being there for a friend that's going through a rough time and having a friend who only drains your energy in every interaction for years on end.

There are two ways to handle this kind of situation. If you think that the person is able to change, then you should have an honest heart-to-heart with them. If they change their ways, then the friendship is saved. However, if they remain the same, then you should go to the next method, which is to distance yourself from that person. Your mental health will thank you.

Romantic relationships

This kind of toxic relationship is one level harder to disinvest from than the first. Let me be clear: any relationship that is physically, emotionally, mentally, or verbally abusive is terrible, and you should leave immediately. However, sometimes, a toxic romantic partner isn't abusive. They may simply lack any motivation and be living in a state of stagnancy, and be trying to keep you there with them.

Our society has told us that we need to have romantic love in order to be happy; this leads many people to fear to be single. They think there is no possible way they could be happy if they were not in a romantic relationship. But if the romantic relationship is stunting your personal growth, it may be time to reevaluate.

Relationships need to be able to evolve and grow. If the person isn't able to evolve, then there isn't much hope for the relationship to be able to survive in the future. As always, make a good-faith effort to speak from the heart and give the person the chance to change their ways. Oftentimes, when romantic partners see their loved one embarking on a journey of self-betterment, they may be inspired to better themselves as well. But if they aren't, and they don't, then you may be better served by disconnecting from an incompatible partner and continuing to grow on your own, rather than be stifled by someone who doesn't want to change.

Family Ties

This is perhaps the most difficult kind of relationship to manage. Family, to some, is the most important kind of connection there is. We put up with things from family members that we wouldn't take from anybody else. That said, while our threshold of patience may be higher for family members, there comes a time when certain behaviors are unacceptable.

Deep down, we know which family members have our best interests at heart. Sometimes there can be teasing or heated arguments, but people come together afterward and apologize and mend fences.

There are some people, though, that does not deserve space in your life, even if you are related by blood. If someone is always making snide remarks and tearing you down for no reason, you don't have to put up with that. Similarly, if a relative condemns you and shames you for simply being yourself, they do not deserve space in your life. Cutting them out may be painful and may cause ripples in your family. However, you must ask yourself: are you willing to sacrifice your own mental health simply to avoid making waves? I'll bet the answer is no.

Relationships can be complicated. Ideally, all of our different kinds of connection, whether they are familial, romantic, or platonic will invigorate us and leave us feeling supported and loved. They may even challenge our ideas, call out our problematic behaviors, and identify ways we can grow as people. But toxic connections will only drain us and decrease the quality of our life. To simplify your life, you need to let them go. Relationships take up a huge amount of space in your life; living a simple life is much easier when you remove people who take up space with negativity, anger, or abuse.

Stressors

Something else that takes up a huge amount of space in our lives is what can be called "stressors." Stressors come from every part of life. They require attention, and we spend a good deal of time and effort handling them. When we pay attention to the things that stress us out, we gain valuable insight into how we are spending our time and mental energy. Some things, like a leaky roof, are important to pay attention to. Other things, like the June Quarterly Report, can take on an unhealthy amount of our time. Paying attention to our stressors can help us evaluate if they are actually worth being stressed over. If they aren't, then maybe we don't need to be giving them so much space in our lives.

Home

Many people view their homes as status symbols. Their homes need to appear a certain way, filled with certain kinds of possessions, and must always meet a certain standard of cleanliness. And there is something to be said for having a floor that is always swept and a home that is free of mess. However, some people take it to the extreme.

There is a common adage of "what will the neighbor's think?" People who have this worry think that the yard has to be weed-free and always mowed, the hedges always perfectly trimmed, and a clean car always parked in the driveway. Worrying about hypothetical neighbors causes us to waste so much time on maintaining boring patches of grass that are laden with chemicals and toxic to bees. It causes us to purchase a certain size television so that the neighbors will be impressed.

Many people spend far too much time worrying about what the inside and outside of their house look like. We only have so much time in the day, and it makes no sense to waste it worrying about something as silly as our lawn.

Work

In the society in which we live, we are taught that productivity is the key to personal worth. The number of things we can get accomplished measures our worthiness as a person. As the great American lie goes, "time is money." Companies demand so much of their employees and usually give so little in return. Your employer wants you to treat your job as the most important thing in your life, but in truth, if you were fired, they could replace you in a week.

We waste so much time investing our thoughts and emotions into our work that we forget about the thing that really matters. Unless you truly love your job and believe you are making the world a better place, your job probably isn't leaving you feeling happy and fulfilled. Of course, it is important to show up to work every day and on time, stay present, and perform to the best of your ability.

But leave work at work. When you come home, there are a precious few hours that you get to yourself or to spend with your family. Make that time count, instead of putting in extra time at the office for the Emergency Du Jour.

Family

The family should be one of the things that bring happiness and joy into our lives. But there are times when things get hectic and out of control that we have to manage. Sometimes, our child gets sick, or we have to take in an ailing parent. These are stressors that we all go through in life.

But sometimes, with family, we can stress ourselves out in ways that are avoidable, unproductive, and clutter our minds and our lives. We may have a tense relationship with a certain person, or another relative may be shaming us for not going with on an expensive family vacation.

We must make a choice to either attempt to repair these relationships or to end them. The only other option is to continue to live in emotional stews that are unhealthy and prevent us from living our lives to the fullest. Not to mention that they stop us from connecting to our family, who are the people that often know us best. Relationships are only valuable as long as they are healthy; this goes even for the family—perhaps, most importantly, for family. Otherwise, it becomes as distracting and useless as a broken vacuum that's been sitting in your living room for the past seven months. It either needs to get repaired or it needs to go.

Extracurricular

We all have hobbies. They allow us to explore our passions and lead a rich, balanced life. However, it should be noted that there is a distinct difference between doing what you love and trying to do it all. We only have so much time, so we have to ensure that we are making the most of the time we do have, which is the very basis of how minimalism applies to life at large.

We need to pay attention to our emotions surrounding our hobbies. We should feel satisfied, happy, or perhaps, challenged (in a good way) by our extracurricular activities. If you notice that something that used to bring you joy now only gives you frustration, it may be time to take a pause and examine the reasons why.

Is it because you simply no longer enjoy the thing you used to love? Or have you simply put so many things on your plate that you are unable to enjoy any of them? As an example:

Ken loves kayaking. He would go out to the river every weekend and enjoy some peace and quiet. He joined a kayak club in order to meet people who shared his interests. Eventually, he was asked to be an organizer for the club. He says yes, and shoulders many new responsibilities. The other person leading the club disappears, and suddenly, he is left with twice the workload.

Suddenly, he is feeling stressed and angry whenever he looks at his kayak and doesn't even enjoy going down to the river on it anymore.

This is a case where something you love can take on a life of its own and you can cease to enjoy it. Ken needs to simplify his life and get back to going down to the river by himself, without any of the extra stressors he unintentionally let into his life.

Set routines and habits

One of the easiest ways for your life to become cluttered with too many obligations is if you tend to operate in chaos. If we never know for sure what our life is supposed to look like, it is all too easy to allow it to become filled with more thing than it can comfortably hold. How, then, do we tame the chaos?

Routines and habits are the death of chaos. Some people may roll their eyes at the thought of establishing a routine. After all, doesn't falling into a routine lead to the death of spontaneity? Don't routines make us boring? Far from it. Having a routine gives our lives comfort and regularity. They allow us to see how much space we truly have in our lives so that we don't end up overfilling them.

Morning and evening routines

When you begin to set routines, the early hours are the best time to start. Having a set procedure for when you wake up in the morning allows you to ease into wakefulness without being jolted or stressed. Setting a routine could be as simple as washing your face, brushing your teeth, and then giving yourself ten minutes of quiet to sit on your back porch and enjoy a cup of coffee.

We've all heard the phrase "wake up on the wrong side of the bed." If we wake up in a bad mood, we have no time to center ourselves before we have to rush through our breakfast and run out the door; thus, this bad mood carries over to the rest of the day. Having time to allow yourself to breathe and center yourself will allow you to shake off the bad mood and prevent it from spoiling the rest of your day.

Similarly, having an evening routine is immensely helpful. A wind-down procedure will signal your body that it's time to start getting ready to sleep, and you will be able to fall asleep easier. Some notes on establishing a nighttime routine:

- Try and get to bed at the same time every night.

- Do not look at any kind of electronic screen at least an hour and a half before bed.

- Do not perform any kind of mentally strenuous activity before bed.

Having a rhythm to your day gives it a flow. It also allows you to carve out small moments of peace where you can anchor yourself and get re-grounded. Having times like this sprinkled throughout your day will lower your levels of stress and raise your overall level of happiness.

Organize your wallet or purse

Another way to set good habits is to ensure that you regularly organize your wallet or purse. When was the last time you actually went through it? Odds are there's a receipt in there from six months ago, as well as a crinkled-up candy wrapper and other assorted trash.

If we're not mindful of these things, we can end up carrying trash around with us for months. What better metaphor for a cluttered life is there, than hauling around garbage that we don't need?

When you organize these spaces, you are saving your future self some time. With less stuff to dig through to find your debit card, driver's license, or glasses case, you'll be able to find the thing you need faster. Not to mention the fact that you're saving yourself a great deal of frustration, an emotion that can quickly clutter up your mind.

Once you begin to practice minimalism in regards to your home, it also makes sense that it will spread to other areas of your life as well. This is a natural outgrowth of decluttering your home. You may even find yourself decluttering other spaces, such as your workspace and your car.

If you have a purse, this is especially pertinent. Empty the entire thing out and lay out all of the items on one large, flat surface. Throw out all the trash. Then go through the items one by one and determine if you actually need them. Be ruthless, and don't keep anything you haven't used in more than a month.

Keep a water bottle with you

This piece of advice may strike you as strange. Why would I tell you to bring an additional item with you, when this entire book has been about telling you to carry less? The answer to that one is easy: you're probably not drinking enough water as it is. None of us are.

Most of us exist in a state of dehydration to some degree or another. This makes our minds cloudy, decreases the efficiency of our bodies, and can have negative long-term health effects. Staying properly hydrated not only helps your body to function better but will help clear your mind as well.

How often have you gotten a pounding headache, seemingly out of nowhere? Odds are, it was a dehydration headache. Not drinking enough water is one of the silliest reasons that we're making ourselves physically uncomfortable, and it is also one of the easiest ones to fix!

So in this case, carry the extra item around with you. Make sure that you're getting at least eight glasses' worth of water every day. Your kidneys will function better, your brain fog will dissipate, and you won't get any more of those pesky dehydration headaches.

It may be useful to set the alarm on your watch or phone to go off every hour, or every few hours, reminding you to drink water. This will help you set the habit of drinking more liquids. Eventually, it will become second nature, and you won't need the alarm anymore.

No phone before bed

We spend so much of our days looking at our phones. We are constantly tied to social media, and spend a huge amount of time scrolling through our feeds on Facebook, Instagram, Twitter, and every other site out there. It fills our mind, saps our mental energy, and takes our attention.

This mental clutter is exactly the kind of thing you want to avoid if you're trying to sleep. When you're trying to drift off, you want a nice and peaceful environment. You want a mind that is untroubled, and you want to spend the time leading up to bed doing some kind of relaxing activity, such as reading a book or knitting.

Obsessively reading Karen's latest Facebook rant, or getting into an argument on Twitter, are the exact opposite kind of thing you want to be giving your attention to. These are time-sucks that demand a huge amount of mental and emotional energy. When you feed them that energy and attention, you are waking up your mind and riling up your emotions.

Is it any wonder that you don't sleep well after scrolling through social media before bed?

Do yourself a favor and set your alarm early in the evening, if you use your phone as an alarm clock. Then set it aside and don't look at it again until morning. Better yet, don't dig into social media and other attention-demanding digital functions until after you've had your morning moment of quiet, and gotten yourself centered and ready for the day.

Learning to say no

This is perhaps the most important skill that you will need to acquire if you wish to simplify your life truly. But learning to say no can be very, very hard. Why is that? As a society, we've been conditioned to learn to say "yes" to everything that comes across our plates. If we say "no," we're afraid of being labeled as someone who isn't a team player, who is stingy with their time, and who doesn't pull their weight.

But if we say "yes" to too many things, then we don't do any of them well. When we limit our commitments, we are able to give one or two things, our full and undivided attention and get great results. But when our attention is scattered between too many commitments, we end up not doing any of them well. Learning to say no is ultimately an act of compassion, not only for yourself but for others. Because if you say "yes" when you aren't able to fully commit, then you're giving their request less than the focus and attention it deserves.

Taking on more than we can handle

We live in a society that has conditioned us to think that our worth is determined by how productive we are. If we aren't able to do All The Things, then we are worthless as a human being. This has led to a toxic mentality where we work so hard, burn ourselves out, and wind up deeply unhappy with our lives. We think that saying "no" is the worst possible sin. After all, we've all heard about those people who said "yes" to every single opportunity for a week, a month, or a year, and how they allegedly live happier, more fulfilled lives.

What worked for those people doesn't work for most of us. Most of us already have too much on our plates and need to work on clearing them off before we pile more things onto them. One of the hardest things about practicing minimalism in your life is learning to decondition yourself to the guilt you have been programmed to feel for denying someone.

People will always want something

No matter who you are, people will always make requests of you. Whether you're a parent who's received the one-millionth request to chaperone a field trip or join the PTA, or you've been asked to take on yet another project at work, the demands will never stop rolling in. There is no world in which the requests will stop coming, so you might as well stop praying for it.

Instead of trying to think of a way to get people to stop asking you to do things, you need to learn how to say "no." The trick is to learn how to stay no in a way that is both compassionate yet firm. Some ways that you can do this are to:

- Frame your refusal as a benefit to them
- Speak from the heart
- Describe the likely outcome if you took on the project, but weren't able to give it the attention it deserves
- Keep it brief
- Keep it kind

Just because you're saying no to someone's request doesn't mean that you're a jerk. Have these conversations as compassionately, yet as firmly as possible. The best case scenario is that the person walks away feeling glad that you were so honest with them, rather than being angry that you refused their request.

When you refuse, ensure that you are showing the person how your involvement in the project would be detrimental to its success at this moment. Reaffirm your relationship and express the gratitude that they thought to come to you with help solving this problem. In the end, you want them to be as grateful that you refused as they would have been if you had accepted.

Setting limits

In order to learn to say no effectively, we also have to learn what our limits are. A good way to do this is first to figure out exactly where your time is going. You may want to time all of your activities in a given week, and then map them out visually on a chart. It may seem like a lot of work up front, but it will give you a visual layout of your time and a birds-eye-view of where all of your hours are going.

Once you know where your time is going, you know what you need to cut out. Do you need to be spending three hours on social media in a given day? Probably not.

But you will also understand just how many commitments you have. Once you understand the true scope of your commitments, take a moment to reflect: do you feel overwhelmed with the amount you have? If yes, you may need to begin offloading them. If no, then you have reached the Goldilocks zone, where you have achieved balance. If you feel as if you are currently not accomplishing much and want a new challenge, it may be time to say "yes" to something new.

Respecting boundaries

Now that you've learned to say "no," you also need to learn to respect other people's "no." Once you have learned to set your own boundaries, you need to learn to recognize and respect other people's boundaries as well. Other people will deny your requests for their time and attention; the key is not to take it personally.

A magical thing happens once you learn to respect other people's boundaries. Once people recognize that you are polite and respectful when it comes to these kinds of requests, when they do say "yes," then their engagement will be that much deeper and more focused, because they understand that you value their time and attention. If you learn to respect others, they will learn to respect you, which remove complicated negative emotions from your life.

Lifestyle

There are a few quick and simple things that you can do to simplify your life right away. Some of the items we've mentioned can be difficult and require a lot of courage. But the ones listed below are quick and easy and can give you some helpful momentum to get the ball rolling.

Unsubscribe from email

We don't just have physical, mental, and metaphorical clutter. We have digital clutter as well. Our email inboxes can cause us a huge amount of stress as soon as we turn on the computer. A quick and easy way to simplify your online experience is to set aside a chunk of time to comb through your inbox.

Pull up your inbox and go through line by line, unsubscribing from any email that you haven't opened. This includes social emails, promotional emails, and spam emails. Be ruthless and be meticulous. Stay at it until the job is done. The odds are that you'll find emails that you didn't even remember subscribing to in the first place.

Don't stay subscribed to any email lists "just in case." Does a company send you promotional emails with discount codes? Great! But have you actually used any of them in the past six months? If not, unsubscribe. Holding onto anything "just in case," even emails, just adds unneeded stress to your life.

Meal prep

Making food should be an act of meditation and happiness as you experiment with new ways to nourish your body. But when you're crunched for time, it can become a huge source of stress. If we're stressed and short on time, we'll make convenient and unhealthy food choices.

This advice can be as simple as making your lunch the night before. If you wish to dive all-in, then you can prep all of your meals for the week on Saturday and Sunday.

Watch less TV

Watching TV can immerse is wonderful stories that expand our horizons. But there is also a lot of trash on TV, and it is stuffed to the brim with companies trying to sell you things.

If you have a few programs that you love, that's fine. But when you watch your program, do so intentionally. And once it's over, turn the television off. Consuming less TV will help to declutter your mind and free up your focus.

Social media

Another egregious time-sucker is social media. It has its place in this modern world—after all, nearly everyone is on it. It's a great way to stay connected with old friends and expand your horizons. But just like with television, be conscious of how long you spend on it.

It is so easy to decide to check your notifications, and then suddenly, you realize that an hour has gone by as you've been scrolling. We spend so much time and emotional energy, arguing our points online. However, we rarely, if ever, can change the opinions of a stranger through the internet. Letting go of the delusion can help to simplify your life.

Set a timer each time you hop on social media. That way, you are holding yourself accountable for the time you spend online.

Make more time for what's important

Once you've cut things out of your life that suck your time, you will be able to critically examine the open stretches of time in your schedule and decide what you want to do with them. Instead of spending two hours a day mindlessly scrolling through social media, you can reclaim that time and decide, mindfully, how you would like to spend that time.

Go back to your core values and bring up your list of intentions. Use these two tools to help guide you in making decisions on how to spend your time. If taming your anxiety is your most important priority, then you will want to spend your time taking up a meditation practice or utilizing some other calming method to give yourself peace of mind. If adventure is your biggest priority, then you can carve out time every day to plan your next one, whether it's as simple as kayaking down the local river or researching and planning your next trip to Nepal.

Living a life that is aligned with your true values is what gives people satisfaction and happiness. The things we do every day all add up to an entire lifetime, so we want to be sure that the things we're adding up are worthwhile. For some people, all it takes to be satisfied is to ensure that they carve out time every single day to enjoy some peace and quiet with a cup of coffee and a good book. For some people, life is a grand adventure, and they need to ensure that they get out and see the world. Whatever your inclination, ensure that you make time for it.

A cluttered life is an unhappy life. We stuff our time full of things we don't need, bought with money we don't have, to impress people we don't like. What's the point of it? We follow a societal script that promises to make us happy, and only leaves us feeling sad and bereft. When we choose to apply minimalism to our lives, we shuck off this script and apply critical thinking skills to evaluate and rethink what we've been taught. And when people realize they don't need things or unhealthy attachments in order to be happy, they become free.

Finances

One of the biggest stressors in our lives is our finances. We live in a capitalist society, which means that we have to earn money in order to keep ourselves clothed, housed, and fed. However, we have learned many unhealthy habits around money in the Western world, and those unhealthy habits are making us extremely unhappy. Some of these habits include amassing huge amounts of debt to buy things we don't need, not paying off our debt, thinking we need to pay large amounts of money for things or experiences, and thinking that we need to have huge, luxurious lives. These are fallacies that will be disproven in the following sections.

Pay expenses when they're due

One of the things that are guaranteed to clutter up your mind, stress you out and complicate your life is if you have unpaid expenses hanging over you. When our bills go past due, we are putting ourselves in a perilous situation. If possible, pay all of your bills not only on time but early. If you have extra money, applying it towards future bills and expenses can save you a huge amount of stress. Instead of worrying at the last minute where the money to pay a certain bill is going to come from, you'll have the comfort and safety of knowing that it is paid up, far in advance.

When your mind isn't cluttered with worrying about which bill has been paid and which haven't, you'll have much more brainpower to apply to other situations in your life. Bills are, by far, one of the most stressful things we have to deal with as adults. If you pay your bills in advance, then you can virtually eliminate that worry from your life altogether.

Do things that are free

We have the mistaken notion in the West that in order for something to be valuable, we have to pay for it. Things that are free are lowbrow, and we appear to be "poor" or "impoverished" if we don't pay huge sums of money for lavish belongings, experiences, or vacations. There's a reason that they say "the best things in life are free."

Instead of paying huge amounts of money to go visit a theme park, you can find many amazing things to enjoy for free, right where you live. Visiting the forest preserves or woodlands near your home is an excellent place to start. Hiking is a great way to challenge your physical endurance, and spending time in nature has been scientifically proven to improve the quality of our mental health. Plus, you get the added benefit of being able to learn vast amounts of information about local plants, animals, and ecosystems. Learning about intricacies of the ecosystems in which we live is a task that can excite any intellect.

If you're not into nature, there are many other things you can do for free or for a very low cost. Give yourself the opportunity to explore them.

Pay down debt

Our society encourages us to acquire debt, but many people end up never paying it down. Instead, they continue to acquire luxury items and apply their money towards small day-to-day luxuries. One of the fastest things you can do to simplify your life is to apply as much extra income as possible towards paying down your debt.

This has many benefits. Firstly, it will vastly improve your credit score, making your financial future much, much easier to navigate. Secondly, you will gain an indescribable peace of mind when you become debt-free. Debt is a shackle that chains us to a system that wants us to buy, buy, buy. Sometimes, we need to acquire debt, such as if we want to buy a house or start a business. But the majority of debt, such as credit card debt, is acquired simply through living the way our society wants us to live.

As anyone who is in debt can tell you, it rules your life. It is a constant pressure on the back of your mind that never lets you fully rest. Once you get out from under your debt, you are in charge of your life again.

Forego status symbols

This is perhaps one of the easiest things you can do to declutter your life. We spend so much money on status symbols to impress other people. However, it's not our job in life to make other people happy; it's our job to make ourselves happy. When you stop trying to impress other people, you are able to live your life for yourself, instead of for others.

You don't need to go fifty thousand dollars into debt for that flashy new car. A reliable used vehicle will serve you just as well. You don't need to spend thousands of dollars on a Caribbean cruise. Getting a cheap AirBnB at some stateside locale with a beach will likely make you just as happy. You don't need to have a however-many-thousand square-foot house. That much space is wasted, plus in the end, you have to clean the entire thing; a smaller condo or cottage may serve you just as well.

In short, status symbols are expensive, flashy, and completely meaningless. There are less expensive options that will stand in just fine, whether it is a house, a car, or a vacation. In fact, downsizing your life may be the right move for you. Selling your gigantic house and moving to a smaller cottage could give you the breathing room you need to finally find the peace that you deserve. Selling the car you only keep in the garage for vanity can give you the money you need to go on an adventure to the other side of the world.

Simplifying your life is never easy. But it is one of the most important gifts that you could ever give yourself. Our culture has conditioned us to feel bad for saying "no," and punishes us for setting boundaries around ourselves and our times. To compound this problem, our fear of scarcity and lack prevent us from letting go of people, things, and opportunities in our lives even if they are toxic and negatively affecting our quality of life. It might be the decades-old friend who has never quite gotten their life together and insists on pulling you down with them. It might be the one small commitment too many that finally becomes the straw that breaks the camel's back. Whatever it is, letting go of things that no longer serve you, though it may hurt or be uncomfortable in the short run, is the only way to ensure long-term happiness.

Conclusion

Thank you for making it through to the end of *The Minimalist And Decluttering Lifestyle.* Let's hope it was informative and able to provide you with all of the tools you need to achieve your goals whatever they may be.

The next step is to pick a room and get started with your decluttering adventure. It may seem overwhelming to start, but that is completely normal! The most important thing to remember is that incremental change is still change. You may only start with one drawer, but eventually, you can simplify your entire life.

As you begin to embody this philosophy, you will be able to use the exercises and methods provided to improve your life. After all, minimalism isn't just about decluttering your house, but about quieting your mind, learning to live in the present moment, and simplifying your life.

Remember that applying minimalism to your life isn't something done in a day, but rather a philosophy that will evolve into a lifelong way of living. Little by little, you can apply the minimalist mentality to clear out unwanted thoughts and stop wallowing in the past or worrying about the future. You can also learn how to make the most of the time you have here on Earth, by learning to compassionately say "no" to opportunities when your plate is already too full.

Finally, if you found this book useful in any way, a review is always appreciated!